A Newcomer's Guide to the United Kingdom

A Newcomer's Guide to the United Kingdom

An insider's guide to getting started and navigating the United Kingdom with ease

Blessing Ashimi and Jackleen Nnely

While every precaution has been taken in the preparation of this book,
the publisher assumes no responsibility for errors or omissions, or for
damages resulting from the use of the information contained herein.

A NEWCOMER'S GUIDE TO THE UK
First edition. June 17, 2023.

For enquiries please contact ashimiblessing@hotmail.com

Copyright © 2023 Blessing Ashimi and Jackleen Nnely.

DEDICATION

This book is dedicated to those who have left their homes and fearlessly ventured into new lands. Your courage inspires us. May this guide be your compass as you navigate the beauty and complexities of the United Kingdom. We respect and admire you as you embrace the challenges and find solace in the shared experiences of others like us.

CONTENTS

Introduction

Before you Depart

    Get your Visa Details Right

    What Should I Travel with?

    Pick the Right Flight

Planning Your Arrival

    Leaving the Airport

    Currency

    Send and Receive Money (Temporarily):

    Your Temporary Accommodation

        Airbnb

        Hotels

Settling In

    What's a BRP? And why do you need one?

    You'll Need a National Insurance (NI) Number.

    Getting a Phone or Sim

    Opening a Traditional Bank Account

    Renting an Apartment

    Getting a Driver's Licence:

Getting a Job

    Volunteering

    Explore Graduate Roles

    Get Certified

    Craft a Winning CV

    Be Strategic in Your Job Search

    Arm Yourself with Knowledge

    Create an Interview Cheat Sheet

    Negotiate Like a Pro

    Do Not Shortchange Yourself

Understand the Essentials

    Healthcare

    The UK Tax System

    Food, Groceries and Supermarkets

    Buying Clothes

    Understand the Weather

    Moving Around

    Language

    Social Life

Final words

About The Authors

Introduction

Moving to a new country is exciting; but it can also be daunting and overwhelming, especially if you don't have the right information to help you navigate your new life. That is where this book comes in; it is your ultimate guide to making a smooth transition to the United Kingdom. Whether you're moving for work, study, or adventure, we will give you all the tips and tricks you need to settle in and start enjoying your new life. From finding the perfect apartment to opening a bank account and even getting a job, this book covers all the essential details you need to make your transition as stress-free as possible. Written from personal experience, it is the resource we wish we had during our big move.

The book is divided into five sections, each designed to help you tackle different stages of your move. Sections one and two focus on what you need to do before you arrive in the UK, including getting your visa, booking the right flight, and packing for your trip. Section three provides tips on what you need to do once you're here, such as setting up your phone, getting a National Insurance number, finding accommodation, and more. Finally, Sections four and five cover some essential information about life in the UK, including finding a job, registering with a GP, the weather, cultural norms, and other important information that you need to know.

The best part? You can read the sections in any order, depending on your situation. And keep an eye out for important tips highlighted throughout the book; they will save you time and help you avoid common pitfalls. So get ready to embark on an exciting new chapter with the help of this comprehensive guide. Moving to the UK has never been easier!

Before you Depart

Get your Visa Details Right

Welcome to the exciting world of moving to the United Kingdom. But before you start fantasising about tea and scones, it's important to understand the intricacies of your visa. I know from personal experience that this can be a bit of a headache. But fear not; I'm here to help you navigate the murky waters of visa regulations.

First things first, it's important to understand the privileges and restrictions that come with your visa. How long are you allowed to stay after your visa expires? Are you permitted to work, and if so, what kind of work and for how many hours? Can you bring your dependents with you? These are all important details that you need to familiarise yourself with. To find this information, you should take a closer look at your visa itself, as well as any emails you may have received from UKVI (that's UK Visas and Immigration) and the UK government website. Trust us, it's worth checking the fine print, as you don't want any surprises down the line.

For most visa types, you'll need to obtain a biometric residence permit (BRP) after your arrival. Don't worry if this sounds a bit stressful; everything you need to know will be explained in more detail later on. So, grab a cuppa (also known as a cup of tea) and get ready to become a "visa expert".

***PRO TIP**: Visa and immigration advice can become outdated overnight due to policy changes. The most authentic source of information is the UK government. Your primary source of information for visas and immigration matters should be their dedicated page at https://www.gov.uk/browse/visas-immigration. If you read anything anywhere that contradicts the UK government, then you know that it's false.*

What Should I Travel with?

Packing for a trip can sometimes be confusing, especially if it's your first time visiting a new country, and you have to consider various factors such as the climate, duration of stay, and, most importantly, what items are permitted on the plane and in the country.

For example, I didn't realise that red meat is not allowed on flights to the UK, which posed a challenge since I had packed some ground beef for my friends. I also did not know that I could bring a pressing iron with me in my check-in luggage. You can bring personal belongings and certain quantities of goods with you without paying UK duty and/or tax. This is known as your *Personal Allowance.*

Personal allowance rules apply to any goods you have purchased overseas and are bringing into the UK, no matter where you bought them. It is important to know these limits and not go over them. If you do, you must declare what you have brought to UK customs before crossing the border. If you bring in a restricted item, this must also be declared. But hold on; don't just pack everything in your luggage yet. Some items are not even allowed.

Now, let's take a look at some of the restricted items. it's a non-exhaustive list, but we've got your back.

- Liquids: You can bring liquids in containers of up to 100 ml, but they must be placed in a clear, resealable plastic bag (up to 20cm x 20cm) and fit inside the bag along with other items. So, make sure you have a clear plastic bag handy in your carry-on luggage for your liquids.

- Medications: If you need to bring medication with you, it's generally allowed for personal use, but some types require a prescription or a letter from your doctor. For instance, common over-the-counter medicines like Paracetamol and flu medications don't require a prescription. However, always double-check with your doctor and the UK customs regulations before you travel.

- Food: You can bring some food items with you, but some have restrictions, such as meat and dairy products. So, if you're a foodie planning on bringing some delicacies with you, make sure to check what you can and cannot bring beforehand.

- Electronics: You can bring your everyday electronic devices like laptops, tablets, and smartphones with you. However, keep in mind that you may be requested to switch them on at some point during your travel, and if your device doesn't turn on when requested, you would not be allowed to take it onto the aeroplane. So, make sure they're charged up and readily available in your hand luggage instead of your checked-in luggage.

- Weapons, illegal drugs, and other restricted items are prohibited.

It is always recommended to check with the airline you are travelling with and the UK Border Force for the latest restrictions and regulations before you travel.

PRO TIP*: You can get most items you need here in the UK, so it is not necessary to fill your luggage with groceries. However, depending on your circumstances, you could travel with essentials that can last you a week or more before you get familiar with your new surroundings.*

Pick the Right Flight

Having an easy travel experience to the UK often depends on what kind of flight you choose and where you sit. Pick the wrong flight with endless layovers, and you have just bought yourself a ticket to misery, so it is important to take the time to research your options. I advise picking a non-stop flight if your budget allows it. With this, there's no second take-off or landing or multiple security checks, and you have less risk of luggage delays or even losing your luggage, which is a major source of frustration for many travellers.

However, if a non-stop flight is not an option, then you should carefully consider the airport you are flying into. Choosing an airport that is closest to your intended destination will make your journey much smoother and more efficient. Avoid secondary airports that are located far away from the city centre or have limited transportation options, as this can add unnecessary stress to your trip. For international flights, many airlines now offer the option to choose your preferred seat beforehand, except for budget airlines. This is a great opportunity to ensure that you have a comfortable and enjoyable flight. I prefer a window seat because it offers less disruption from people walking by and I have the view to enjoy. You should also avoid sitting next to the toilet, as it could get very smelly on some flights.

It is also good to consider the timing of your flight, particularly if you prefer a less crowded experience. Midweek flights tend to be less busy compared to weekends and public holidays, so this can be a good option for travellers who wish to avoid crowds. By considering these tips, you can greatly improve the ease and enjoyment of the flight.

PRO TIP: *During takeoff and descent on my first flight, I felt something like a pop in my ears, which led to ear pain for a few days. This is called an "Airplane ear" and can be quite uncomfortable. It usually occurs due to a change in ear pressure. Airplane ear can be alleviated by chewing gum or yawning during descent or takeoff.*

Planning Your Arrival

There's a famous saying that goes, ***"By failing to plan, you are planning to fail."*** This saying is a constant reminder that it is always important to plan every little detail about a trip, especially when it's a big move such as migrating to a new country. One aspect of your trip that needs extra planning is your arrival, so we will focus on covering the essentials and laying some groundwork. This will ensure, as much as possible, that your first few hours in the UK are enjoyable and incident-free.

Leaving the Airport

As a newcomer to the UK, you'll likely be bringing a significant amount of luggage with you. While this might sound great at first, carrying heavy luggage around can quickly wear you out and put a damper on your mood. To avoid this, it's advisable to plan your exit strategy from the airport with your luggage in mind.

I would suggest taking a taxi to your destination, provided the cost is reasonable. You're probably familiar with popular taxi companies such as Uber and Bolt, and they're readily available in the UK. With their respective apps, you can easily make a booking and enjoy a hassle-free ride. Alternatively, there are multiple taxi operators around the airport that you can use if you prefer. Keep an eye out for them or simply ask for assistance if you need it, but do keep their cost in mind as they can sometimes be more expensive to use, especially if you are travelling to a city far away from the airport.

If you do opt to travel by public transport, such as a train or a bus, you can book your tickets online in advance. Just be sure to read the ticket terms properly before purchase, as some tickets are non-refundable and cannot be used for another time slot in case your flight gets delayed. It's also important to keep in mind that border control processes at UK airports can sometimes take a while; you could be in the queue for hours, so if you're planning to book train or coach tickets in advance, be sure to factor in enough time for border control when selecting your travel time. You don't want to miss your scheduled departure because you're still waiting in line at border control. It is better to be safe than sorry, so double-check the terms to avoid any disappointment.

The good news is that the UK has an excellent transport system, which should make your journey to your destination relatively straightforward. Whether you're travelling by train or bus, you should be able to get to where you need to go without too much fuss. You could also pre-plan your journey and determine the most efficient route to your destination. To do this, you can use the Transport for London (TFL) website. The TFL website provides a wealth of information on the various modes of transportation available in the UK, including the Tube, buses, and trains. You can access the TFL website at www.tfl.gov.uk and enter your starting point and destination. The website will then provide you with the most convenient and cost-effective routes, as well as travel times and any necessary transfers.

For the lucky ones who have friends or family offering to pick you up, take advantage of their kind gesture. Having someone you know on hand can be incredibly helpful, especially if they are familiar with the area. They can guide you to your initial destination with ease, making your arrival in the UK a lot more comfortable and enjoyable.

Currency

As with any society, you'll need some local currency to spend. If you have a working debit or credit card, you will be able to make purchases conveniently around the UK, as most places accept card payments. Plus, using your card to make purchases often comes with the added benefit of receiving better exchange rates than if you were to use a bureau de change. However, bear in mind that some smaller businesses may still require cash payments. This could include food trucks or even barbershops, as one of us has personally experienced this. For this reason, it is a good idea to bring some cash along with you, as a form of fallback strategy. I recommend coming along with at least 500 pounds in cash, if possible.

You will be able to withdraw cash at the airport or nearby ATMs; just be sure to check with your bank or card provider before you travel to avoid any unexpected foreign transaction fees or restrictions on your account. And speaking of restrictions, it's important to consider any restrictions your local banking authorities may have placed on your card. Some banks may have limitations on international transactions and how much you can spend. This could cause issues when using your card to make purchases abroad.

PRO TIP*:*

Always stay up-to-date with news regarding your bank and foreign currencies to avoid any surprises while travelling. Currency exchange rates, banking policies, and international transaction fees can change frequently and unexpectedly, so it's important to keep an eye on any updates or news related to your financial institution.

Send and Receive Money (Temporarily)

As soon as you set foot in the UK, you will quickly find out that your lifestyle will be limited without a bank account. You may be able to open a bank account in your home country, but this might be impractical for some. Hence, I will advise you to use a virtual account until you are fully settled.

There are multiple options, the most popular being Monzo, TransferWise, and Revolut. These are digital wallet apps that issue virtual accounts in multiple currencies, allowing you to send money across the world at very competitive rates. We can personally vouch for TransferWise (now rebranded as Wise), and our experience has been stellar. Not only will you be issued a UK bank account that you can use to send and receive money for free, but you'll also get a debit card sent to your UK address in five days or less! Plus, you can start using your virtual card right away to pay for items online while you are waiting for the physical card to arrive. However, there's a caveat: TransferWise and Revolut are e-money institutions approved by the UK Electronic Money Regulations, but they are not banks. What this means is that the e-money or payment services that these organisations provide are not covered by Financial Services Compensation Scheme protection (FSCS), so if they ever shut down, your money goes with them. We'll get into this in detail in the next chapter.

Your Temporary Accommodation

Unless you're fortunate enough to have friends or family who can offer you temporary accommodation, finding a place to call your own is a top priority when starting your new life. Luckily, there are several great options when it comes to deciding where to stay:

Airbnb

This is an excellent option if you prefer an apartment-like setting without the obligation of a long-term agreement to tie you down. Airbnbs vary in price, and you can easily find one to suit a reasonable budget. Bear in mind, though, that as with any apartment you rent without seeing it physically, Airbnb can be a mixed bag. Pictures and descriptions can be misleading, leaving you with an undesirable place to stay. You should not make any assumptions if you don't want surprises. Ask your host about the basic amenities before you book. Does the heating work? Is WiFi included? Can I cook if I want to? Are there any rules I need to be aware of? What is your policy for early or late arrivals? Some of these questions might already have answers on the Airbnb listing; be sure to ask if not.

If things go wrong, you can contact Airbnb for help. But bear in mind that getting a new place at short notice can be a huge headache, and it will cost you much more than it should have, especially if you're on a tight budget. So, take the time to do your due diligence before you commit to anything.

Hotels

Booking a hotel is one of the easier options, provided you can afford the kind of hotel you like. Websites like Agoda.com and Booking.com are excellent places to begin your search for hotels and apartments because they offer a great selection, but it's important to read the terms and conditions as some bookings may have non-refundable fees or hidden charges. To avoid falling into that situation where your money "hangs", choose the free cancellation option. This gives you more flexibility in case your travel plans change. In cases where you need accommodation as soon as possible, you could consider using the services of tour companies at the airport. Their prices are often inflated, so this may not be the best option.

When you arrive at the airport, the border patrol could also ask you where you will be staying, so it is advisable to print out your booking and have it nearby when you arrive at the airport. On arrival at your hotel, ensure that you have your international passport on hand, as this is usually the most widely accepted form of identification. Whatever option you eventually settle for, booking well in advance can save you significant amounts of money.

Compare prices online and read reviews from other travellers to get an idea of the hotel's level of comfort, cleanliness, and service. Also, make sure the location is safe and convenient for your journey.

Settling In

What's a BRP? And why do you need one?

Obtaining your Biometric Residence Permit (BRP) card should be your top priority when you arrive in the UK. A BRP card is a document issued by the UK government to non-European Economic Area (EEA) nationals who are living in the UK for a period longer than six months. The card serves as proof of the holder's immigration status and right to work, study, or access certain public services (but not public funds) in the UK. You shouldn't lose it, as you can't do much in terms of setting up your life in the UK without your BRP card.

Details regarding where you will pick up your BRP card will be emailed to you by the UK government. Typically, it will be a post office located near the UK address you provided during the visa application process. All you need to do is go to the designated post office and collect your BRP card. Sometimes, delays in collecting your BRP could occur due to backlogs by the UK government; in such cases, you would be informed, so do not fret.

Important BRP Update:

While at the time of writing, the BRP card is the de facto proof of immigration status, the Home Office intends to stop issuing BRP cards on January 1, 2025. This is due to its plans to digitise the immigration system as much as possible. Visa holders will then rely solely on their digital status to demonstrate their rights

You'll Need a National Insurance (NI) Number.

In the UK, people who are allowed to work legally are given a National Insurance (NI) number by the government. This unique number is very important for keeping track of the taxes that an employed person pays into the National Insurance system, which funds various state benefits, including the National Health Service (NHS) and state pension. Having an NI number is very important, as all working people who are subject to tax must have one. Employers typically require job applicants to provide their NI number, and some may not hire someone who does not have one. I lost a job offer because there were delays with my

NI number and the employer did not accept my application reference number, which some employers deem valid provided you update this information when you finally receive your NI number. So, you see, NI numbers are not to be joked with. If you are residing in the UK and have the right to work, you will need a NI number if you are employed, searching for work, or have received a job offer. Obtaining a NI number involves two steps: applying online and verifying your identity, which can be done either online or in person. Detailed information about the application process can be found on the UK government website.

It's also worth noting that some visa categories do not require or utilise a NI number. If you already have an NI number, you won't need to apply for a new one, even if your details change, since your number will remain the same for life. Interestingly, some BRPs (Biometric Residence Permits) have the NI number printed on their back, although this is dependent on factors such as the issue date and visa status.

Getting a Phone or Sim

One of the things I love about the UK is the phone plans. Phone plans in the UK typically include a combination of call minutes, text, and data allowances. Some phone plans here are pay-as-you-go, meaning you could top up monthly and cancel at any time, but some phone plans are contracts where you'll have to commit to a set period, which could be anywhere between 12 and 24 months. Before selecting a phone plan, consider what your usage patterns are. For example, do you tend to use more data, text, or make more calls?

Getting a phone plan can either be done online or in-store and should be relatively straightforward. There are tons of plans and providers to choose from, as the UK has several major providers. If you already have a phone or don't want to be locked into a long contract, then a pay-as-you-go option from a provider such as GiffGaff or Lebara may be a good option. They offer competitive prices and SIM-only plans with flexibility in terms of what they offer. You could also shop around and compare prices and plans to see which one offers the most value for money. It is always a good idea to read the terms and conditions carefully to ensure that you understand what is included in the plan and what any additional costs might be. Some providers might not be upfront with hidden clauses, and most providers would charge you a cancellation fee, so always read the terms and conditions before you commit to any plan.

PRO TIP:

Many people assume that to get a sim-free phone contract in the UK, you need to have a credit history or have lived in the country for at least a year. However, this isn't always true. Websites like fonehouse.co.uk can provide you with a phone contract even if you have only been in the UK for a month. Just resist the urge to apply online and give them a call instead to discuss your options.

Opening a Traditional Bank Account

As you navigate the UK financial landscape, you'll find that there are a number of banks offering various financial products to suit your needs. From current and savings accounts to mortgage and credit card options, the banking industry has something for everyone to choose from.

If what you need is an account for everyday use, a current account is your best bet. However, opening a bank account in the UK can be a bit of a challenge if you don't yet have a stable address. Most banks require proof of address to open an account, which can be a utility bill, rental agreement, or other document that proves your residence in the country. For those who don't yet have these documents, mobile banks like Starling and Monzo are a good fallback option, as their verification requirements are easier to fulfil. However, there is always a way. If you're in the UK for school or work, your university or employer should be able to assist you with opening a bank account, which would eliminate the need for these strict documents. In terms of keeping your money safe, the UK government regulates the financial system to protect customers through the Financial Conduct Authority (FCA) and the Prudential Regulation Authority (PRA). These bodies are responsible for ensuring that banks operate safely and provide fair services to everyone who banks with them.

There are also differences between the types of banks available. For example, popular banks like Lloyds Bank offer traditional banking services such as branch services as well as virtual services, while mobile banks like Starling and Monzo provide services exclusively online and are also protected by the UK bank deposit protection scheme called the Financial Services Compensation Scheme (FSCS), which protects individual depositors' savings up to £85,000 per depositor should the bank go out of business. So depending on your needs, you might want to choose the most suitable bank for you. I like banks with branches, especially when I have to make large deposits, as I do not care for post office deposits. I also need a physical brand to hold them accountable should I have any issues with their services, so a mix of both traditional and virtual banks works great for me.

Renting an Apartment

Renting an apartment is an excellent option if you are seeking a more long-term stay or prefer the flexibility and independence that come with having your own space. However, the stress that comes with finding an apartment in the UK is not often talked about. For those unfamiliar with the housing market, it can be an emotional rollercoaster. Despite this, there are various options available that can meet your specific needs, including traditional apartments, studio apartments, detached and semi-detached houses, and house shares. Also, there are several agents who can assist you in your search for a home that fits within your budget. It is important to carefully consider your needs and preferences when choosing a type of property, as each option offers its own unique set of features and benefits.

Once you've decided on the type of property you're looking for, the next step is to start your search. There are several ways to do this, including searching online, contacting a letting agent, or walking into any letting agency near you. It's also a good idea to check out property websites, such as Rightmove, Zoopla, or Spareroom (for flatshares). They have a wide range of properties available for rent. From my experience, Spareroom tends to be easier if you are new to the UK, as most letting agents will ask you for a reference from your previous UK landlord, which you won't have at this point. Facebook groups for the area you are interested in are also a good resource but beware of scams.

You will need to have a clear idea of what you can afford. Rent prices vary widely depending on location and property type, so set a realistic budget and stick to it. Once you have found a property that meets your needs and budget, the next step is to submit a rental application, or offer, as most agents like to call it, which typically involves providing personal information such as your name, address, education details if you are a student or employment details. You will also need to have your passport or ID card at hand. Most times, landlords receive multiple offers and just go with the one who's willing to move in fast or who they have more confidence in. One valuable piece of advice I received from an agent is to always specify how quickly you are willing to move into a property. The faster, the better.

It is equally a good idea to show your ability to afford the property by declaring your current or expected income, particularly if you are employed or if you have a job offer and can prove it. In today's challenging housing market, it is not uncommon for renters to opt to pay three to six months' rent in advance to secure a property. While paying six months' rent upfront may be excessive, if you have been searching for a property for a while and have the means to do so, offering to pay some months' rent in advance can be an option. Only take this step if you are confident that the property is genuinely the one you want and not out of desperation to secure any apartment. Interestingly, in my experience, there have been times when the landlord declined the upfront payment and still offered me the property. This happened twice, and both apartments were lovely. So do what works for you and your budget.

Once you have successfully secured the property, as part of the rental process, you will be asked to provide a security deposit. This deposit typically amounts to four to five weeks worth of rent. By law, the landlord is required to place this deposit into a tenancy deposit protection scheme that is approved by the government. This safeguard helps to ensure that your deposit remains secure in the event of any disputes that may arise.

On top of that, you will also need to sign a rental agreement, which outlines the terms and conditions of the tenancy, such as the duration of the tenancy, the rent amount, and any other fees or charges. Agreement types vary, so check what you are getting into carefully. The common ones are a tenancy agreement, a sublet agreement, and a lodger agreement. A tenancy agreement means your name is on the lease or rent; for a sublet, you are paying someone else who has rented the apartment; for a lodger agreement, you are simply staying temporarily, and you have next to zero rights. These agreement types won't mean much until something goes wrong.

If you are renting for more than a few weeks, do not sign a lodger agreement, as they end up becoming a nightmare.

A few more things to note here:

- Never pay for an apartment you have not seen. Scammers will usually try to get you to pay a deposit or the rent without seeing the apartment.

- If it looks too good to be true, it probably is. Rental scams aren't uncommon in the UK, and you need to be careful not to fall victim.

- Confirm with the landlord if the deposit will be placed in a deposit protection scheme and which one. If not, run!

- As a tenant, you have certain rights and responsibilities. For example, you are responsible for paying rent on time and maintaining the property in a clean and tidy condition.

- You have the right to live in a property that is safe and secure and to expect the landlord to carry out necessary repairs and maintenance.

- Do not dry your clothes indoors, as you'll attract mould to the property, and you might end up losing your deposit. Your landlord might also ask you to pay for additional damages.

Getting a Driver's Licence:

To drive in the UK, one must meet certain age requirements. For cars and motorcycles, the minimum age requirement is 17, whereas, for larger vehicles like lorries and buses, the minimum age requirement is 21. If you hold a valid driver's licence from your previous country of residence, you are allowed to drive in the UK on that licence for 12 months from the date on which you became a resident, that is, the day you landed in the country. A special "International Driver's Licence" is not required during this time, as I've seen many people waste their funds getting an international driver's licence when a regular driver's licence would suffice. So do not waste your money. When your one-year period elapses, you will need to apply for a provisional licence and complete the UK's practical driving test.

Drivers who hold licences issued in countries that have an agreement with the UK, known as "designated countries", including Andorra, Australia, Barbados, the British Virgin Islands, Canada, the Cayman Islands, the Falkland Islands, the Faroe Islands, Gibraltar, Hong Kong, Japan, Monaco, New Zealand, the Republic of Korea, the Republic of North Macedonia, Singapore, South Africa, Switzerland, Taiwan, Ukraine, the United Arab Emirates, and Zimbabwe, are eligible to exchange their licence for a UK licence within five years of their arrival.

If you hold a valid licence issued by a European Union or European Economic Area country, you are permitted to drive in the UK until the licence expires, and there is no need to retake the driving test.

PRO TIP:

It is advised that you opt for the tracked package when sending your application for a provisional licence. By doing so, you can rest assured that your request will be given priority treatment, as it will be delivered directly to someone at the office instead of being dropped off with a pile of unsorted mail. This ensures timely delivery and reduces the risk of your application being lost or delayed. You can apply for a provisional licence at www.gov.uk/apply-first-provisional-driving-licence.

Getting a Job

When embarking on the job search journey in a new country, it is necessary to brace yourself for the possibility that your expectations may not align with reality. Some individuals may have the luxury of securing a job before their arrival, providing a smoother transition, while others may have to rely on their enrollment in a university or their dependence on a partner with a study or work visa. Although each individual's situation may differ, the common thread that unites everyone is the universal need for employment.

It is also not unusual for a newbie seeking information to come across advice from immigrants on various online platforms, describing the difficulties they faced in pursuing their career aspirations. Many of these narratives express the need to start with menial or low-level jobs before climbing the ladder towards more desirable jobs. While this may hold true for some, it is not always the case. The outcome of your job search is ultimately dependent on your unique goals and the approach you take to achieving them. That is not to say that just because a job is considered "low-level", it suddenly means that it is a demeaning job. There's great dignity in all forms of labour, regardless of the pay grade. If a short-term gig that pays the bills is what's available to you, there's no shame in holding onto it. However, if you're feeling stuck and yearning for something more fulfilling, then this chapter is definitely up your alley.

In this chapter, we'll provide you with a comprehensive roadmap that has proven to be successful for countless individuals in their pursuit of gainful employment as new immigrants. By following the steps outlined in this guide, you'll be equipped with the necessary tools and resources to potentially land a high-paying job that aligns with your professional ambitions.

Volunteering

Volunteering with organisations that are hiring for positions that interest you can be an excellent way to gain relevant experience, develop new skills, and also have that "UK" experience on your CV. This is especially true for students or individuals who are looking to switch fields, as it can be challenging to gain relevant experience without any prior work history. Volunteering allows you to gain practical experience while also providing you with the opportunity to network with professionals in the field.

One of the main advantages of volunteering is that it can help you stand out as a candidate when applying for paid positions. Employers are often impressed by candidates who have taken the initiative to volunteer in their industry and demonstrate a willingness to learn. Volunteering can also help you develop essential skills that are highly valued in the workforce, such as teamwork, communication, and problem-solving.

While it is important to note that volunteer roles are unpaid, the experience and knowledge gained from these positions can be invaluable in the long run. Additionally, volunteering can be an excellent way to give back to the community and contribute to social causes. There are several websites that can help you find volunteer roles that align with your interests and skills. Reachvolunteering.org.uk and volunteermatch.org are two popular sites that offer a wide range of volunteer opportunities. It is also worth checking out LinkedIn and Indeed, which often list volunteer positions alongside paid roles.

In essence, volunteering can be an excellent way to gain valuable experience, develop new skills, and make a positive impact on society. While it may not provide immediate financial gains, the experience gained from volunteering is an investment in your future career. By volunteering with organisations that align with your interests and goals, you can position yourself as a strong candidate for future paid positions.

Explore Graduate Roles

Graduate roles can be an excellent option to consider when starting in a new field, especially as a student. Many companies also offer their own graduate programmes. These programmes provide a structured pathway for new graduates to develop their skills and gain work experience, which often leads to permanent roles. They often include a combination of training, mentoring, and practical work experience, allowing graduates to develop a broad range of skills and knowledge.

One of the easiest ways to find graduate roles is via job sites such as MilkRound, Bright Network, Indeed, Reed, Total Jobs, and LinkedIn. These job sites offer a wide variety of positions across multiple industries and provide you with the ability to filter by location, industry, and salary to find roles that match your skills and interests.

When searching for graduate roles, ensure you tailor your application to each specific role and company. Research the company and read the job description carefully to understand what they are looking for in a candidate. Craft your application to highlight relevant skills and experience and demonstrate your enthusiasm for the role and the company. Many graduate programmes have a competitive application process, so ensure that your application stands out from the crowd by showing the employer the value you bring, and the best way to do this is in your cover letter. Never skip a cover letter for a graduate job application, as it sets you apart.

Get Certified

Having a certification in your field can be a major advantage in positioning yourself as a qualified candidate for a particular role, especially in the UK, where employers in their respective fields highly value these certifications and many others because they set a clear standard for excellence. Certifications also demonstrate your commitment to ongoing learning and professional development, as well as your mastery of specific skills and knowledge areas that are relevant to your profession.

One key advantage of certifications in the UK is that they can give you a competitive edge when applying for jobs. Many employers require or prefer candidates who have specific certifications, especially in fields such as Tech, Healthcare, and Engineering. Having a certification on your CV can set you apart from other candidates and demonstrate your expertise and dedication to the field.

Certifications can also help you advance in your career in the UK. For example, if you are in Tech, certifications such as the British Computer Society's Chartered IT Professional (CITP) or Microsoft Certified Solutions Expert (MCSE) can help you move up the career ladder and take on more complex roles with higher salaries. In Healthcare, certifications such as the Nursing and Midwifery Council's Registered Nurse (RN) or the Royal College of Physicians' Membership (MRCP) can open up new career paths and increase your earning potential.

Another advantage of certifications is that they provide a standard of excellence and set a benchmark for your skills and knowledge that is recognised in the UK. Employers know that candidates with certifications have met rigorous standards and have demonstrated a certain level of proficiency in their field. This can give employers confidence in your ability to perform well on the job and meet their expectations.

Certifications can also provide ongoing professional development opportunities and keep you up-to-date with the latest trends and technologies in your field in the UK. Many certification programmes require continuing education or recertification, which ensures that you stay current with changes in your field and continue to develop your skills over time.

Examples of certifications in the UK include the Association of Chartered Certified Accountants (ACCA) for accounting and finance professionals, PRINCE2 Foundation and Practitioner for Project Managers, and Certified Information Systems Security Professional (CISSP) for IT security professionals.

Craft a Winning CV

Updating your CV is a critical part of any job search, and make sure that your CV is tailored to the role you are applying for. One way to do this is to think about what you accomplished in your previous roles and highlight the skills and experience that are relevant to the position you are applying for. It can also be helpful to search for job ads in your desired field and look for common requirements and qualifications. By infusing some of the buzzwords from these job ads, you can ensure that your CV includes relevant keywords and phrases that are likely to catch the attention of hiring managers and recruiters.

Another tip for crafting a strong CV is to avoid including your location. It is no longer necessary to include your city, state, or even country on your CV. Instead, simply leave your location as "United Kingdom", as this will ensure that your CV is not overlooked due to potential biases or assumptions about your location.

When it comes to the formatting of your CV, keep it clear, concise, and easy to read. The Harvard template is a popular choice among job seekers, as it provides a clean and professional look that is easy to customise to your specific needs. But know that there is no one-size-fits-all approach to CV formatting, and you should choose a template that best suits your style and the role you are applying for.

One general rule of thumb when it comes to CV length is to keep it to one page or at least two pages maximum. This will ensure that your CV is easy to read and highlights the most important information about your skills, experience, and achievements. I have years of work experience, but I prefer my CV to be a single page. This is because I include a link to my LinkedIn profile on my CV, where interested employers can find more comprehensive details about my past roles and responsibilities. This approach is based on my personal preference, and you should choose a format that suits your individual needs and showcases your qualifications. In summary, do what works best for you.

Be Strategic in Your Job Search

Once you have been in your voluntary role for around 4 to 5 months, it is a good idea to start thinking about your next steps and how you can leverage your experience to land a paid job in your desired field. One effective strategy is to sign up for job search sites like Glassdoor, Reed, and Indeed, which can help you find relevant job opportunities and apply for positions online.

When applying for jobs, you should highlight your relevant skills and experience and demonstrate how your past experiences have prepared you for the job. Remember to include any transferable skills you have gained or even the tools you can use, such as Power BI, SQL, Tableau, MS Project, etc., depending on your skills or field of interest.

In addition to applying for jobs, you would need to practise your interview skills. Even if you don't get the job, each interview is a valuable learning opportunity that can help you refine your approach and better understand what employers are looking for. Before each interview, research the company and the role thoroughly and prepare answers to common interview questions. Be ready to provide specific examples of how you have demonstrated the skills and experience required for the job, and be prepared to ask thoughtful questions of your own. Never leave a job interview without asking questions.

If you receive a rejection, don't get discouraged. I got a lot of rejections when I first moved to the UK, but I did not let that stop me from applying for more jobs. Rejections are a part of life and a normal part of the job search process, and each rejection brings you one step closer to finding the right fit for you. Use any feedback you receive to improve your approach and make yourself a stronger candidate for future opportunities.

You also have to approach your job search strategically. Personally, during my job search, I treated the process of applying to job postings as a full-time job. I made it a daily habit to apply to at least five or more job openings. Do not get fixated on the number of applications, though, as it is the quality of your applications that matters. It can be helpful to broaden your search by applying to multiple organisations and actively seeking out hiring managers or recruiters on LinkedIn. Sending a brief and polite message along with your CV could increase your chances of catching their attention, even if they don't respond. This proactive approach can help you stand out in the job market.

Arm Yourself with Knowledge

One effective way to learn more about your industry is to take advantage of the abundance of resources available online. Watching YouTube videos, listening to podcasts, and reading industry blogs can be a great way to stay informed and up-to-date on the latest trends and best practices in your field. But you need to remember that not all content is good content, especially with so much information available. It can be easy to become overwhelmed or confused. Especially with so many "noisy experts" out there who recycle information without facts just to gather views, you have to ensure that the content you are consuming is of high quality and comes from reputable sources. So search for podcasts hosted by industry leaders or YouTube channels created by professionals with extensive experience. Reading industry blogs or newsletters from well-known experts can also be helpful.

Once you have identified high-quality resources to learn from, you could also create a learning plan and stick to it. Schedule time in your day or week to watch videos, listen to podcasts, and read articles on topics relevant to your field. As you become more knowledgeable about your field, you can use this expertise to your advantage during interviews and when speaking with potential employers.

In addition to learning from online resources, it can also be helpful to connect with other professionals in your field. Join industry-specific groups on social media, attend networking events, job fairs, or conferences, and seek out mentorship opportunities. A friend of mine attended a job fair that Barclays attended; he got the details of a new role and shared them with another friend who applied and got a job with the organisation. So you see, your network is your net worth.

Create an Interview Cheat Sheet

When preparing for a job interview in your field, you can anticipate the questions that are likely to be asked. One effective way to do this is by creating a cheat sheet that contains common questions and answers. This will help you to be more confident and well-prepared during the interview.

To create your cheat sheet, start by researching the job position and the company you are applying to. Look for information about the company's culture, values, and mission statement. This will give you an idea of what the employer is looking for in a candidate.

Next, make a list of the questions that are likely to be asked during the interview. These may include questions about your experience, skills, strengths, weaknesses, and ability to handle certain situations. You can also look for common interview questions online and tailor them to your specific field.

For example, if you are applying for a software engineering position, some common questions may include:

- Can you explain your experience with programming languages X, Y, and Z?

- Can you walk me through how you solved a particularly challenging programming problem?

- How do you stay up-to-date with the latest technology and trends in the software engineering field?

- Can you provide an example of a project you worked on that required teamwork and collaboration?

- Can you explain how you handle project management and prioritisation?

Once you have identified the questions, draft your answers clearly and concisely. Use bullet points or short paragraphs to organise your thoughts. Practise answering these questions out loud to help you remember your responses and feel more confident during the interview.

In addition to the typical interview questions, employers may also ask situational or behavioural questions to assess your problem-solving skills and ability to handle challenging situations. The STAR method is a useful tool to use when answering these types of questions.

The STAR method stands for Situation, Task, Action, and Result. Here's how it works:

- **Situation:** Describe the situation or problem you were faced with.

- **Task:** Explain the task or goal that needs to be accomplished.

- **Action:** Describe the specific actions you took to address the situation or achieve the goal.

- **Result:** Share the outcome of your actions and what you learned from the experience.

By using the STAR method, you can provide a clear and concise response that demonstrates your skills and abilities. This approach also helps you stay on track and avoid rambling or getting off-topic during your response. Remember to own your story and be confident as confidence is key.

Negotiate Like a Pro

It can be intimidating to negotiate salary expectations during a job interview but do not shortchange yourself and do your research ahead of time. One useful tool is to search for the company on job search websites like Indeed and Glassdoor to find out what they typically pay their employees for the specific role you are applying for.

When researching salary rates, be sure to look for companies that are similar in size, industry, and location. This will give you a more accurate benchmark to use when discussing salary expectations during the interview. Once you have gathered this information, be clear and confident when discussing your salary expectations. During the interview, the employer may ask about your expected salary or salary history. Do not rush by stating a figure; instead, ask them what their budget is or if there is a salary range they are looking at. This way, it gives you leverage to call a higher figure and negotiate better. However, if they hesitate to mention a figure, then be honest and transparent about your expectations and provide the benchmark you found during your research.

For example, you could say something like, "*Based on my research on the industry and this specific role, I believe a fair salary range for this position would be between X and Y. However, I am open to discussing this further based on the specific details of the position and the overall compensation package.*"

Remember that negotiating a salary is a normal part of the job search process, and it is okay to ask for what you believe you are worth. The employer is looking for the best candidate for the job, and if you can demonstrate your value and experience, they will likely be willing to negotiate with you. Always approach salary negotiations with a positive attitude and a willingness to compromise. Be prepared to discuss other aspects of the compensation package, such as benefits, vacation time, and bonuses. These can also be negotiable and may help offset a lower salary offer.

Do Not Shortchange Yourself

One misconception about moving to a new country as a skilled professional is the assumption that one has to start from scratch in their field. This is not necessarily true. A professor once told me that Africans sometimes undervalue their skills and go for lower-paid roles due to a lack of confidence or the fear of rejection. I understand that it is not always easy to find a job in a new country, especially for a senior position, as you may feel like your qualifications and experience are not recognised or valued in the new job market. However, you have to remember that many employers value diverse experiences and skill sets, also rejections are a part of life and it has nothing to do with your race or background. I once heard a story from a friend about someone who had a strong interview performance for a position. However, when asked if she had any questions for the hiring managers, she made a comment implying that she believed she wouldn't be hired due to her race and nationality. Unfortunately, she didn't get the job, not because of her race or nationality but because her pessimism and subtle accusation of bias undermined her confidence. It is important not to assume that all companies are biased and instead approach opportunities with confidence and a positive mindset, regardless of preconceived notions about race and how others may perceive you.

If you have a high level of skill and managerial experience in your field, you have much to offer potential employers and you have to show it. By leveraging your existing experience and qualifications, you can find roles that are a good fit for your skillset and background. To begin your job search, start by researching the job market in your new country. Look for companies that are similar in size and industry to those you worked for in your previous country. This will help you identify job openings that match your skillset and experience.

When applying for managerial roles, you have to emphasise your leadership and team management experience. This may include highlighting your experience managing teams, setting goals and objectives, and developing and implementing strategies. During the interview process, be confident and assertive in discussing your experience and qualifications. Emphasise your ability to bring a fresh perspective and diverse set of skills to the company.

Also, ensure that you continue to develop your skills and experience in your new country. This may include taking additional courses or certifications to enhance your skill set and stay current with industry trends and best practices.

PRO TIP: *Reach out to employees of companies you are interested in on LinkedIn, as many companies pay for referrals. When you do ask for a referral, be specific about the role you're interested in by sharing a link or a screenshot of the role and why you think you would be a good fit. Provide any relevant information about your skills and experience, and offer to share your CV for their review.*

Understand the Essentials

Healthcare

Living in the UK means that you have access to one of the most comprehensive healthcare systems in the world, the National Health Service (NHS). The NHS provides healthcare to all residents of the UK, regardless of their income, and is known for its free-at-the-point-of-service principle. This means that you don't have to pay any fees to see a doctor, nurse, or any other healthcare professional.

The NHS is made up of a network of general practitioners (GPs) and hospitals that provide a wide range of medical services. GPs, also known as family doctors, are usually the first point of contact for most medical issues. They offer a broad range of general medical care, including diagnosing and treating illnesses, prescribing medications, and making referrals to specialists. You can register with a GP practice near your home, and you will usually see the same doctor each time you visit; in some cases, you may have to book a call back from a GP, depending on your hospital. In case of an emergency, the NHS provides 24/7 emergency care for serious and life-threatening illnesses and injuries. Accident and

Emergency (A&E) departments are located in most hospitals, and you can show up without a prior booking. NHS emergency services can be accessed by dialling 112 or 999.

Although the NHS is renowned for providing quality healthcare, waiting periods for minor circumstances can be long and sometimes frustrating. Appointments can take anywhere from two weeks to three months, depending on your health challenges. However, if you ever find yourself experiencing intense pain or discomfort and your scheduled appointment is still a few weeks away, you have the option to visit A&E without prior booking. You can simply show up, and a doctor or nurse will attend to you promptly.

The NHS isn't the only way to get health care in the UK. There is also a private healthcare sector. Private healthcare is not free, and individuals usually pay for it through private medical insurance or out-of-pocket expenses. Private healthcare can offer quicker access to medical services and treatments, but it may come at a higher cost.

The UK Tax System

Every new immigrant would need to understand the country's tax system and their obligation as a taxpayer. The UK has a progressive income tax system, which means that the more you earn, the higher the rate of tax you'll pay. Here are a few key things to know about taxes in the UK:

- **Tax residency**: To be considered a tax resident in the UK, you must be present in the country for 183 days or more in a tax year (6 April to 5 April of the following year). If you are considered a tax resident, you will be required to pay taxes on your worldwide income and gains.

- **Taxable income**: In the UK, most forms of income are taxable, including wages and salaries, rental income, and investment income. You will also be required to pay taxes on any foreign income you bring into the UK. Depending on your circumstances, other taxes may apply to you, such as Capital Gains Tax, Inheritance Tax and council tax.

- **Self-assessment**: The majority of people in the UK are required to complete a self-assessment tax return each year, which must be submitted by January 31. You'll need to provide information about your income, deductions, and tax credits to calculate your tax liability.

- **National Insurance Contributions**: In addition to income tax, you will also need to pay National Insurance Contributions (NICs) on your earnings. NICs are used to fund the UK's social security system and provide access to benefits such as state pensions.

One notable aspect of the UK's tax system is that individuals who earn £12,570 or less in a given tax year are currently exempt from paying any income tax. This exemption is made possible through a mechanism called the "personal allowance", which serves as a tax-free threshold for individuals. The personal allowance is the amount of income an individual can earn before they start paying income tax. For the tax years 2021-2022 and 2022-2023, the personal allowance in the UK stands at £12,570. If an individual's annual income is equal to or less than this amount, they fall under what is commonly referred to as the "tax-free bracket."

In practical terms, it means that individuals who earn £12,570 or less are not required to pay any income tax on their earnings. This allows low-income earners to retain their entire income, providing some financial relief and assistance.

However, this exemption applies specifically to income tax and does not cover other types of taxes such as National Insurance contributions or other taxes related to specific circumstances or income sources. It's also worth mentioning that the personal allowance can change from one tax year to another, as it is reviewed and adjusted periodically by the UK government to account for economic factors and changes in the cost of living. So individuals need to stay informed about the latest tax regulations and thresholds to accurately determine their tax obligations.

***PRO TIP**: At the time of writing, the figures quoted above were accurate. See https://www.gov.uk/income-tax-rates for up-to-date information on income taxes.*

Food, Groceries and Supermarkets

When it comes to food, the UK is a melting pot of flavours and influences, drawing inspiration from diverse communities. With a wide range of traditional British dishes, international cuisine, street food, and local delicacies, the UK's food culture is a feast for the senses. From the iconic fish and chips to the comforting shepherd's pie, traditional British food has stood the test of time and continues to be a firm favourite. Of course, taste is subjective, and what may be delicious to one person might not be to another. However, if you're willing to explore and embrace new flavours, you are sure to find something to tantalise your taste buds in the UK, as the country's international cuisines have something for everyone. You are sure to find a restaurant from your home country or a store that sells food items from your beloved country. So, whether you're a lover of tradition or a food adventurer, don't miss out on the opportunity to experience the diverse and delicious food culture that the UK has to offer.

Now let's talk about the supermarkets. With supermarkets in the UK, there's no shortage of options. But if you're new to the country, it can be confusing to choose where to shop. So, let's take a closer look at some of the most popular supermarket chains in the UK and what makes them unique.

1. **Tesco**: Tesco is currently the largest supermarket chain in the UK, with stores located throughout the country. They offer a wide range of products, including groceries, fresh produce, and household items, at relatively low prices.

2. **Sainsbury's**: Sainsbury's is the second-largest chain of supermarkets in the UK and is known for its focus on quality and fresh produce.

3. **Asda**: Asda is a popular supermarket chain known for its low prices and wide range of products. Asda offers fresh food, groceries, clothing, and home and leisure goods.

4. **Morrisons**: Morrisons' business is predominantly food and grocery-focused, with a significant portion of it sourced locally. There's also a world's food aisle at Morrisons, where you are sure to find food items from all over the world.

5. **Aldi and Lidl**: These are German discount supermarkets that have a strong presence in the UK. They offer a limited range of products, but they tend to be cheaper than other supermarkets.

6. **Waitrose**: Waitrose is known for its high-quality products, particularly fresh produce and organic products.

All these supermarkets offer a wide array of products, including groceries, fresh produce, household items, and their own-brand products. They also offer services such as online ordering, click-and-collect, and home delivery. Additionally, many supermarkets in the UK offer fuel stations, pharmacies, and other services. So, whether you're a bargain hunter or a foodie, there's a supermarket in the UK that will cater to your needs.

PRO TIP: *If you crave delicacies or products from your home country, be sure to check the "World Foods" or "Internationals" sections of supermarkets. They usually stock products from various communities around the world, e.g., African, Asian, Oriental, Caribbean, and many more.*

Buying Clothes

The UK is home to a wide range of clothing options, from high-street fashion to designer labels and even charity shops. The UK provides a wide range of opportunities for individuals to express their style. Let's explore the various avenues for purchasing clothes in the UK and offer tips on how to find the best deals and unique pieces.

1. **Designer Labels:** The UK is known for its vibrant high-street fashion scene, with major cities like London, Manchester, and Edinburgh housing stores that cater to different styles

and budgets. From well-known brands like Topshop, Zara, and H&M to department stores like Selfridges and Harvey Nichols, high-street fashion offers trendy and affordable options for fashion enthusiasts. Affordable designer items can also be bought at outlet stores such as Bicester Village, London Designer Outlet, or even stores such as TK Maxx for a steal.

2. **Charity Shops:** For those seeking unique and affordable finds, charity shops in the UK provide a treasure of clothing and household items. Organisations like the Salvation Army, British Red Cross, and Cancer Research UK run these shops, offering second-hand clothing that is often of high quality and at low prices.

3. **Primark and Budget-Friendly Alternatives:** When it comes to affordability, Primark is a household name in the UK. With numerous stores across the country, Primark offers a vast selection of clothing, accessories, and home goods at budget-friendly prices. Their fast-fashion approach allows individuals to keep up with the latest trends without breaking the bank. While Primark is a popular choice, there are also other budget-friendly alternatives available, such as New Look,

ASOS, everything5pounds, and Boohoo, which cater to a wide range of styles and budgets.

4. **Off-Season Shopping:** An insider tip for savvy shoppers in the UK is to take advantage of off-season sales. By planning your purchases strategically, you can snag incredible deals on clothing for all seasons. For instance, a good tip for weather changes is to buy your winter outfits during the summer and vice versa, as they are usually a lot more affordable during off-seasons since these clothing brands typically reduce prices to make room for new stock.

Understand the Weather

The United Kingdom has a temperate maritime climate with cool summers and mild winters. The weather can be unpredictable, varying from day to day. Rainfall is common throughout the year, with fog and mist being frequent occurrences. The northern and western regions of the UK tend to be cooler and wetter than the south and east. The warmest months are typically June, July, and August, while the coldest months are December, January, and February.

The UK's Met Office issues weather warnings for events such as heavy rain, snow, and high winds. Heeding these warnings can help you prepare for any potential disruption to your plans.

***PRO TIP**: Never leave home dressed based on how you feel or what you think. Check the weather forecast and dress appropriately.*

Moving Around

One of the most popular ways to travel in the UK is by train. The country has an extensive rail network that connects major cities and towns, making it easy to travel between destinations. Train travel is often faster than driving and can be more convenient, as you can sit back and relax while enjoying the scenery. Another popular option for getting around the UK is by car. If you prefer to have more control over your itinerary and the flexibility to explore at your own pace, then renting a car is a great choice. The UK has an extensive road network, including motorways and A-roads (major roads that link regional towns and cities), making it easy to get around. However, be prepared for traffic congestion in major cities and towns, especially during rush hour. Also, driving in cities such as London can be manic, and beware not to break any rules as you would get fined instantly. My first time driving in London, I mistakenly drove on a bus lane, and I had to pay a fine of £80, so don't be like me.

For those looking for a more budget-friendly option, bus travel is a great alternative. Most cities and towns in the UK have regular bus services linking them to other destinations. Bus travel is generally less expensive than train or car travel and can be a good option for shorter journeys.

PRO TIP: *Except within city centres, beware of relying on buses at night, as service can be quite unreliable. If there's a reason for the bus not to show up, it won't. My personal experience anyway!*

Language

Though English is the country's official language, different regions of the UK have distinct dialects and accents, and it is key to be conscious of these differences. Even if you've spent your entire existence communicating in English, there is a possibility that initially, you will have trouble understanding what is being said. This is perfectly normal, and your hearing will get used to it eventually.

To help speed up this adjustment period, there are a few things you can do. First, make an effort to listen to English-language media, such as TV shows, movies, and podcasts. This will give you exposure to a variety of different accents and dialects. Also, don't be afraid to ask others to repeat themselves if you don't understand what they are saying. Most people will be happy to accommodate you and will appreciate your effort to understand them. I must confess, I still don't understand the Manchester accent. Maybe if I eventually move to that part of town, then I will; who knows?

Social Life

The UK has a diverse and vibrant social scene, with many opportunities to socialise and make new friends. This can vary depending on the location and community, but several common elements make up social life in the country. One of the most iconic aspects of UK social life is its pub culture. Pubs, or public houses, are traditional gathering places for people to socialise, have a drink, and enjoy a meal. Many pubs also host live music and other events, making them a popular destination among the locals. Another popular aspect of UK social life is sports. Football (soccer) is particularly popular in the UK, and many communities have a local team that people support. Additionally, there are many other sports, such as rugby, cricket, and tennis, that are also popular in the UK.

The UK is also known for its nightlife, with many cities and towns offering a wide range of options for entertainment and socialising. You can also find events happening near you through a quick Google search. But be careful and stay safe, as crime rates vary between cities.

PRO TIP: *You can use apps like Meetup to find communities and events that interest you. Churches, mosques, and other gatherings are also excellent places to meet like-minded people.*

Final words

As our time together comes to an end, we hope this guide has provided you with a comprehensive understanding of life in the UK. From its rich cultural heritage to its diverse population, there is so much to explore and discover. But perhaps the most important thing to take away from this guide is that the UK is a place of great opportunity and growth, no matter where you come from. Whether you are here to study, work, or settle down, the UK welcomes you with open arms. As you venture out into this exciting new world, remember to keep an open mind, be respectful of the people and their customs, and embrace the challenges and opportunities that come your way.

And with that, we wish you all the best on your journey in the UK. May it be filled with adventure, growth, and success

About The Authors

Blessing Ashimi is a Software Engineer with a unique blend of experience spanning multiple industries. Before relocating to the United Kingdom in 2022, He worked in the travel and tourism industry for over four years. A mathematician by training, Blessing's passion lies in problem-solving and exploring new cultures.

Jackleen Nnely, a Project Manager in Nigeria, embarked on her journey to the United Kingdom in 2021 to pursue a Master's Degree in Project Management at the University of Northampton. She currently works as a Senior Project Manager at an infrastructure engineering software company in the United Kingdom. Jackleen is also passionate about linking newcomers to new opportunities by giving them the tools to succeed through her non-profit platform, Immigrants in Tech. In her free time, Jackleen enjoys binge-watching shows on Netflix and immersing herself in African literature.

Printed in Great Britain
by Amazon